Swedish Beauty Secrets

Other books by PAAVO O. AIROLA:

- HOW TO GET WELL
- WORLDWIDE SECRETS FOR STAYING YOUNG
- ARE YOU CONFUSED?
- HOW TO KEEP SLIM, HEALTHY AND YOUNG WITH JUICE FASTING
- CANCER: CAUSES, PREVENTION AND TREATMENT – THE TOTAL APPROACH
- STOP HAIR LOSS
- THERE IS A CURE FOR ARTHRITIS
- HYPOGLYCEMIA: A BETTER APPROACH
- THE MIRACLE OF GARLIC
- EVERYWOMAN'S BOOK
- THE AIROLA DIET AND COOKBOOK

BOOKS BY PAAVO O. AIROLA
are available at all better health food stores and
book stores

Swedish Beauty Secrets

How to feel and look healthier, younger
and more beautiful

by PAAVO O. AIROLA, N.D., Ph.D.

HEALTH PLUS, Publishers, Sherwood, Oregon

SWEDISH BEAUTY SECRETS
Copyright © 1974 by
Paavo O. Airola, N.D., Ph.D.

All rights Reserved. No part of this publication may be reproduced or transmitted in any form or by any means, electronic or mechanical, including photocopy, recording, or any information storage or retrieval system now known or to be invented, without permission in writing from the publisher, except by a reviewer who wishes to quote brief passages in connection with a review written for inclusion in a magazine, newspaper, or broadcast.

8th printing, completely revised edition, May 1993

Published by
HEALTH PLUS, Publishers
P.O. Box 1027
Sherwood, Oregon 97140

ISBN #0-932090-07-9
Printed in the United States of America

Table Of Contents

Introduction 3
Chapter 1 The Secret of Rose Hips 5
Chapter 2 The Secret of Whey 15
Chapter 3 The Secret of Home Beauty Care 23
Chapter 4 Natural Internal Cosmetics 29
Chapter 5 Natural External Cosmetics 33
Chapter 6 Beauty From Within 43

INTRODUCTION

In a faraway northern Scandinavian country lies a vast treasure of beauty secrets used for many years to enhance and promote natural beauty. From Sweden, have come many women possessing the radiant, natural beauty desired by women throughout the world. In fact, the export of glamorous stars to the world of entertainment has been well documented. Stars such as Greta Garbo, Ingrid Bergman, Inger Stevens, Signe Hasso, Maj Zetterling, Anita Ekberg, Ann-Margaret, May Britt and Britt Sellers are a few of the familiar names.

Visual observation alone will attest to the fact that Scandinavian women seem to have clear, beautiful complexions and a healthy glow superior to other women of the world.

Is it a coincidence that Sweden consistently produces some of the worlds most beautiful women? What secrets of health and beauty do Swedish women have that are hitherto unknown to others? Can certain natural internal and external cosmetics actually promote a more beautiful complexion and enhance appearance? These are questions this book will answer, as well as give you the most important information regarding natural cosmetics.

I have had the opportunity to live in Sweden for many years and have researched the lifestyles, nutritional habits and beauty rituals of Swedish women. I have come to the conclusion that the acknowledged beauty of Swedish women is not an unrelated coincidence. For centuries Swedish women have used certain elements in their daily diet and beauty care regime which the latest scientific research has proven to be of great benefit in our quest for a more youthful and healthy appearance. This book is a compilation of those "Swedish Beauty Secrets".

Chapter 1

The Secret of Rose Hips

The beautiful rose is without doubt the queen of the flower kingdom. From time immemorial the rose has been the symbol of romance and beauty. It has been the inspiration of poets and artists. The delicate natural fragrance of the rose is extracted and made into perfumes and beautifying rosewaters. Rose-petal extract has been used by beauty conscious women around the world for centuries.

Swedish women have discovered yet another beauty-enhancing secret within the rose. They eat the rose. Yes, the fruit of the rose, called a rose hip, has been a daily addition to Scandinavian diets for hundreds of years. Today, the rosehip continues to be an important part of the daily diet in Sweden.

Rose hips are the fully-ripened orange-red fruits (about the size of a cherry) just below the rose flower. They develop after the rose drops its petals, but the "hips" do not begin to mature into a fully ripened fruit until the cooler weather of fall arrives. They are picked in the late fall, just before the frost destroys them. All roses have "hips", but only certain species of the rose have a fruit suitable for food. *Rosa Villosa* and *Rosa Canina* are two fruit-bearing varieties of roses which are grown predominantly in cold northern climates. The most common fruit-bearing variety in the United States is *Rosa Rugosa*. In Scandinavia there are wide areas covered with wild rose bushes from which Swedes pick "hips" in the fall.

Rose hips are used very extensively in the Swedish diet. Swedes make nutritious soups, delicious teas, jellies, and other desserts from them. Rose hips in Sweden positively do not have the flair of a fad-food about them. All Swedes use rose hips. They are sold in various forms in all food stores and are a staple food in the humble cottage as well as in the king's castle. If you dine in the finest Swedish restaurant, or lie as a patient in a Swedish hospital, you will more likely than not find rose hips in some form in the menu.

Now, why should Swedes eat rose hips? And what does all this have to do with their beauty? Rose hips have been an internal beauty aid to Swedish women for years, and it has been only recently that this knowledge has been understood.

VITAMIN ROSES

Rosehips are sometimes called "vitamin roses", and they most certainly are! Rose hips contain more vitamin C than any other known natural source - twenty to forty times more than oranges!

In the cold northern climates, the availability of vitamin C-rich foods are limited, even in the summer months. Foods such as tomatoes, green peppers, cherries, and many others, do not grow well in the short growing season of Scandinavia. Imported citrus and other vitamin C-rich foods, are expensive and not always available. The people of those regions have been relying on rose hips for their source of vitamin C as a matter of necessity.

Here's how rose hips compare with oranges:

- They have 28% more calcium.
- They have 25% more iron.
- They have 25 times more vitamin A.
- They have 20 to 40 times (depending on the variety) more vitamin C.

Rose hips are also rich in bioflavonoids, as well as many other vitamins and minerals. The Bioflavonoids, such as citrin, hesperiden, and rutin, are abundant in rose hips as a companion nutrient to vitamin C. These two vitamins always occur together in foods and for good reason. Recent research has proven bioflavonoids to be essential for the efficient absorption of vitamin C as well as protecting the vitamin C molecule from oxidation. The main function of bioflavonoids is to increase the strength of the capillaries and regulate their permeability. Through support of the capillaries, bioflavonoids increase the delivery of oxygen to the tissues, and the elimination of wastes from the tissues. In this way, bioflavonoids are directly involved in maintaining the health of collagen.

Most of us are aware of the indispensable value of vitamins C and A for health. They are used in the treatment of colds, infections, skin disorders, and many other diseases. Vitamin A has long been associated with the health of the skin. Many beauty-conscious women have been using vitamin A preparations and foods rich in vitamin A (carrot juice) to enhance their complexion. But how many have thought of vitamin C as absolutely indispensible for a healthy and youthful complexion?

There are, of course, many other factors involved in feeding and maintaining a healthy skin, such as vitamin B-complex, minerals, and essential fatty acids. But the breakdown of collagen, caused by deficiency of vitamin C, is the main cause of the deteriorating processes of the skin and the primary contributing cause of premature aging.

COLLAGEN - KEY TO PERPETUAL YOUTH

Scientific discoveries (by Drs. J.W. McCormick, Johan Bjorksten, and others) have shown that the aging processes and the degenerative changes of the skin, such as wrinkles, flabbiness, discolorations, etc. are caused by physiological changes in collagen - the intercellular cement substance. This deterioration is affected primarily by the deficiency of vitamin C in the tissues. The integrity of the collagen must be maintained in order to give support and shape to the body and to maintain healthly blood vessels. Sufficient vitamin C in the diet will keep the collagen strong and elastic, which will result in a tight skin and a smooth and lovely complexion.

Collagen, the substance which holds the cells together, is responsible for the stability and the tensile strength of practically all the tissues of your body, including the skin and muscles. The deficiency of vitamin C brings about the breakdown of this intercellular cement, and, as a result of this, the instability and the fragility of the tissues. In plain language, if you are deficient in vitamin C, in addition to the other symptoms of weakened health, your skin becomes loose and soft, it loses its tension and elasticity and it becomes saggy and lifeless. That is why your eyes lose their luster, your lips their fullness, and your chin drops down. That is why the skin on your arms and legs becomes flabby and loose.

THE IMPORTANCE OF VITAMIN C

Two hundred years ago, Captain James Cook was the first to recognize the importance of vitamin C in maintaining good health. Although he didn't know vitamin C was the micronutrient which miraculously saved his crew from sickness and death, he insisted that they eat fresh foods throughout their journey. These fresh foods, such as cabbage and potatoes, prevented the disease known as scurvy.

In 1911 scurvy was officially recognized as a disease caused by a dietary deficiency of vitamin C. Since the time of it's first discovery, vitamin C has gained additional recognition for the importance it plays in maintaining overall good health and vitality.

Much research has been done that documents vitamin C as the most miraculous natural substance involved in promoting health and preventing disease. For example, vitamin C has been shown to have preventative effects on hypertension as reported in the "International Journal For Vitamin and Nutrition Research". The British medical journal "The Lancet" has reported that there is a substantial relationship between vitamin C and the cardiovascular system. Vitamin C plays an important role in the prevention of high cholesterol levels.

According to Dr. W.J. McCormick, an international expert on vitamin C, vitamin C deficiency is related to a diversity of ailments such as the common cold and other viral infections, hernia, cervical lacerations, pre- and post partum hemorrhage, rheumatism, arthritis, tuberculosis, pneumonia, spinal disk lesions, hardening of the arteries, and other circulatory changes.

Dr. Glen King, renowned nutritionist, stated that vitamin C deficiency causes decreased urinary excretion, anemia, greater susceptibility to infection and subcutaneous hemorrhage in joints and muscles. Many of the above disorders are basically due to the loss of integrity of collagen. Vitamin C is also necessary for the utilization of iron. Iron-deficiency anemia, or course, will have a devastating effect on the vital functions of the body as well as the complexion.

Two German doctors, Professor Werner Grab and Professor H. Kraut, attribute great curative powers to vitamin C. Hepatitis, influenza, rheumatic diseases, metabolic diseases, polio and acute poisonings are helped dramatically with vitamin C treatments. Dr. Grab has stated that even cancer will be inhibited by huge doses of ascorbic acid (vitamin C).

In Russia, where much research has been conducted on the benefits of vitamin C, doctors prescribe vitamin C for many conditions of ill health. Rose hips are cultivated in the colder northern climates and are used as teas and soups in the daily diet.

The world-famous Nobel Prize winner and Vice-President of the "International Society for Research on Nutrition and the Diseases of Civilization", Dr. Linus Pauling, shocked the world of organized medicine by announcing that he "discovered" the cure for the common cold - vitamin C. He said that he and his wife, both susceptible to frequent colds previously, have taken 3,000 mg. of ascorbic acid each day for the last 5 years and did not contract a single cold during this period! According to Dr. Pauling, a tenfold increase in the daily intake of vitamin C will bring about an increase in both physical and mental well-being. The optimal daily dose for most people should be ten times the recommended dose of 75 mg. Daily ingestion of 3 to 6 grams of ascorbic acid leads to increased vigor, and increased protection against infectious diseases, including the common cold. In addition, the body's ability to heal in times of distress, such as injury or illness will be greatly enhanced.

From cancer prevention to wound healing, from high cholesterol to hypertension, researchers around the world have documented the nutritional benefits of vitamin C. Unfortunately, reports from the U.S. Department of Health have indicated a growing problem of vitamin deficiency in the U.S. Many American families eat diets deficient in vital nutritive elements. Vitamin C has been found to be one of the most deficient substances in the

American diet due to the easy availability of highly processed foods and "fast foods". Vitamin C, being heat sensitive and susceptible to oxidation, is difficult to obtain from processed, prepared foods. Even processed orange juice contains very little vitamin C, primarily due to the prolonged high heat used to produce it. That is why it is vital to eat fresh foods rich in vitamin C in your daily diet.

What Swedish women have known and used instinctively for hundreds of years has now been confirmed scientifically and acknowledged by the worlds leading scientists. Recent research has proven vitamin C to be indispensable in the treatment of many conditions as well as necessary for the maintenance of optimum health.

Centuries ago, Swedish women knew nothing about vitamin C or its effect on health or on the complexion. Perhaps it was intuition that drew these women into the forests to pick the fruits of wild rose bushes. In the cold northern climates of Scandinavia, where few fresh fruits and vegetables grow, rose hips became an essential food element, providing not only vitamin C but an increased resistance to disease and a beautiful fresh complexion as well.

Perhaps it is understandable now why the symbol of beauty, the rose, brings beauty to Swedish women. By using rose hips, the magic fruit of the rose, in their daily diet, Swedish women have been constantly beautifying themselves, by keeping their collagen strong and solid, their skin tight and elastic, and their complexion smooth and fresh looking. The rose truly has brought not only beauty to the women of Sweden, but increased health and vitality as well.

Chapter 2

The Secret of Whey

Whey has been a staple food of the Swedish people throughout history. It is consumed daily in the form of delicious *mess-öst* and *mess-smör*. You can buy them in every food store and you find them on every table. *Mess-öst* is a whey cheese and *mess-smör* is a whey butter.

What is whey? During the cheese-making process, milk is coagulated, which causes the separation of the solid portion of the milk from the liquid portion. This liquid is called whey. In the U.S. this thin semi-clear liquid is often sold as a by-product for animal feed. It is also dehydrated and the resulting powder is sometimes used as an ingredient in bakery products. In Sweden, whey is never an ingredient in animal feed because it's nutritional value is highly esteemed. Therefore, it is made into cheese and butter and consumed as commonly as our own cheese and butter is in this country.

In earlier times, when the dairy was neither industrialized or mechanized, all dairy products were made directly on the farms. Whey butter and cheese were made by boiling whey in large kettles over the fire until the water evaporated and the semi-solid whey remained. Then the whey was put into cloth and wooden forms to harden into whey cheese. It was also put into glass jars and mixed with cream to form a butter-like spread called whey butter. Even now, in some parts of Sweden, whey cheese and whey butter are made by the farm women in this primitive way. However, most whey products in Sweden today are made in the modern dairy factories by modern evaporating processes.

What value does whey have in promoting beauty? Research has revealed the following interesting facts. An efficiently functioning digestive and eliminative system has a profound effect on not only overall health and well-being, but the prevention of premature aging as well. The lack of fiber in the diet is the major cause for disorders of the digestive tract which leads to such ailments as constipation, colitis, diverticulitis, and even cancer of the colon. Whey contains certain elements that contribute to the overall health of the digestive and eliminative systems. However, before examining whey and its benefits, it is important to understand how these systems function and the significance diet plays in keeping these systems healthy.

THE SECRET OF ETERNAL YOUTH

For thousands of years man has searched for methods to extend his life and prolong his youth. Of all the "secrets" of perpetual youth which man has tried, there is one which has been scientifically established to promote health and well-being and therefore possibly a longer and more youthful life. It is based on the premise that the colonic hygiene - or the perfectly and efficiently functioning digestive, assimilative and eliminative system - is vital to the overall health and youth of the body.

Ilja Metchnikoff, the eminent Russian bacteriologist, made revolutionary discoveries at the turn of the century in regard to ways of prolonging life. He believed that auto-toxemia (self-poisoning) through putrefaction of metabolic wastes in the large intestine was the main cause of premature aging.

Your intestines house billions of bacteria which help your digestive system break down the food you eat and thus aid in the digestion and assimilation of nutrients. Some of these bacteria are called "the friendly bacteria", like the acidophilus, and bifidus; some are called "unfriendly", which are putrefactive bacteria.

For optimum health it is imperative that there is a good balance between these bacteria. When your diet is unbalanced, as in the case of too much animal protein and over-refined constipating foods, the balance in the intestinal flora will be disturbed. Harmful, unfriendly bacteria will take over and the result will be sluggish bowels, gas, putrefaction and constipation. The toxins, or poisons, created by bacterial metabolism and putrefaction, remain in the intestines and, as a result of prolonged constipation, are absorbed by the blood system and, consequently, poison the whole body.

Many scientists believe that chronic intestinal sluggishness and self-poisoning, together with faulty nutrition and deficient assimilation of food, are the major contributing factors of premature aging.

Nothing is more devastating to the beauty of complexion than internal sluggishness and constipation. A serious constipation problem will cause the complexion to take on a muddy gray tone, feeling rough and porous and often covered with eczema, pimples, and other blemishes. Of course constipation can also be detected by the presence of bad breath. This kind of bad breath cannot be washed away with mouthwash because its origin is the stomach and the lungs. The lungs are an important detoxifying organ. When the intestines are constipated, putrefactive wastes accumulate and impurities then enter the bloodstream. The lungs will then attempt to cleanse the blood as it passes through and the result will be bad breath.

YOGURT AND WHEY

The popularity of yogurt as a rejuvenating health food and beauty food is based on the following physiological facts:

- Yogurt helps to restore the bacterial balance in the intestines.
- Yogurt promotes the growth of the friendly bacteria and helps to combat intestinal putrefaction and prevents constipation.

It has been empirically demonstrated that the soured milk or yogurt-eating people of Bulgaria, Russia, and other East European, and Balkan countries live longer and enjoy youthful vitality throughout their long lives.

A very important part of the Swedish diet is *filmjölk*, or a soured milk very similar to yogurt. The highly sweetened, fruit flavored yogurts so popular in the U.S. cannot be found in Sweden. Rather, their version is a pure unprocessed form of cultured milk which contains beneficial bacteria. Many Swedes enjoy a bowl of *filmjölk* for breakfast, and eat whey products in the form of cheese with the evening meal, thereby naturally providing a daily ritual of cleansing their intestinal tract.

Whey and yogurt possess very similar qualities, whey being a somewhat more concentrated form. Whey is 77% pure lactose, which is a natural food for the friendly acidophilus bacteria in the intestines. It has been scientifically established that using whey regularly will prevent internal sluggishness, gas, bowel putrefaction and constipation. Whey will prevent the growth of the putrefactive bacteria.

In addition to being an internal cleanser, whey helps to establish a better, healthier condition in the whole digestive tract, and helps in the assimilation of nutrients. It is particularly helpful for the retention of minerals in the system, especially calcium, an essential mineral for the promotion of a beautiful complexion. Moreover, it helps the system in the manufacturing of certain B-vitamins in the intestines.

Whey is useful not only because of its miraculous cleansing effect on the digestive tract. Whey is also an excellent food. It is rich in minerals, particularly in iron, and vitamins, especially the age-fighting vitamin B_1. Here are a few nutritional facts about Swedish whey cheese:

- 77% of whey is pure lactose - the active factor in its favorable influence on the intestinal tract.

- Whey cheese contains only 3.6% butter fat as compared with 25-30% for ordinary cheese.
- The amount of B_1 is 10 times higher in whey cheese than in ordinary cheese.
- The amount of B_2 in whey is 7 times higher than in beef.

THE IMPORTANCE OF B VITAMINS

The importance of B vitamins cannot be underestimated in keeping our skin healthy and beautiful.

It has been shown that deficiency of vitamin B_1, or thiamine, will cause premature aging, depression, insomnia, skin irregularities and hives. Thiamine regulates and normalizes oxidative metabolism by means of its function of transforming glucose to energy, thereby protecting against oxidation.

Deficiency of vitamin B_2 produces sores around the mouth, cracks in the lips and has been blamed for the typical and very unbecoming symptom of aging, disappearing lips. This is the condition where previously full lips begin to diminish in size and eventually become very narrow, almost disappearing totally.

Pantothenic Acid, a part of the B complex, is of specific importance to women who wish to delay the aging process. Through studies, done at the University of Texas by Dr. Roger J.

Williams, it was found that pantothenic acid is a powerful anti-stress vitamin. Stress has been shown to be a contributing factor in a variety of disorders, as well as contributing to aging. Pantothenic acid is a constituent of co-enzyme A, which is involved in energy metabolism. It is essential for the production of adrenal hormones, especially cortisone, which can protect against every form of stress. It has been reported that gray hair returned to its normal color when pantothenic acid was taken together with other B vitamins, especially PABA, biotin, and folic acid.

PABA and folic acid are two vitamins that play a key role in preventing premature aging. They are both involved in keeping the glands working effectively, increasing virility and vitality. Folic acid is essential for protein synthesis, production of DNA and RNA, and cell division and regeneration. PABA has some antioxidant activity. It also protects against exposure to ozone. Both PABA and folic acid are also anti-stress factors and anti-graying agents.

In addition to whey, the best natural sources of B vitamins are brewer's yeast, whole grains, fresh raw wheat germ, raw nuts, sunflower seeds, green leafy vegetables, rice bran, peas, beans, milk and milk products. Incorporating these foods in your diet will help to assure that you obtain all these vital nutrients thus promoting a beautiful, youthful appearance.

Chapter 3

The Secret of Home Beauty Care

In addition to the two most important beauty aids - rose hips and whey - the lovely, clear and luscious complexions of Swedish women are favorably affected by alternating temperature changes.

Swedes are outdoor, sporty people. They live in a rugged climate with severe and rapidly changing temperatures. Their skin is exposed to constant temperature changes, as they spend much of their time outdoors - skiing, skating, swimming, hiking, riding, etc. They swim in ice cold water in the winter, often directly after a hot steam bath.

There is a unanimous agreement among the foremost experts on beauty and health that constant temperature changes are invigorating and stimulating on the biochemical activity of the skin. Fresh cool air and outdoor activities stimulate blood circulation and bring more blood to the outer layers of the skin.

Outdoor activities and sports increase the supply of oxygen to every cell of the body, speed the metabolism and accelerate the activity of the endocrine glands. The secret of youthfulness and femininity lies in active glands, healthy collagen, and good flow of nutritive-laden blood.

If you live in a climate which is not conducive to rugged outdoor activities, here are a few ways to stimulate your skin which you can practice in your own home.

NATURAL SKIN STIMULANTS

Warm and Cold Treatments

Once or twice a day, take an alternate warm and cold shower, preferably in connection with your daily exercises. Start with warm water and make three to four changes from warm to cold during each bath. Specifically, expose your face to the cold and warm changes. Always finish with cold water and rub yourself dry and warm with a coarse towel.

Rinse your face with cold water several times during the day. This can be done anywhere: in your house, in your office, at your place of work - just walk to a washroom and with the palms of your hands, splash your face a few times with cold water, then dry it by patting gently with a paper towel. Then look in the mirror and see how your face has acquired a new, healthier look; how your complexion becomes rosier, tighter, more beautiful, more alive. This simple routine, if you let it become a habit, will do more for your beauty than all the most elaborate and expensive cosmetics in the world.

When sunbathing, don't expose your face to the hot sun for more than 10 to 15 minutes. Exposure to the sun is very damaging to your skin and can cause premature aging. If you stay in the sun for several hours, alternate your sunbathing with swimming in cold water, or take a cold shower, or rinse your face with cold water now and then. Be sure to protect your skin from the harmful effects of the ultraviolet rays of the sun by using an appropriate sunscreen designed to provide maximum protection.

Swedish Facial Sauna

Swedish facial sauna is a very effective treatment for blackheads, pimples, acne, and for the thorough cleansing of your face.

Take a tablespoon of your favorite herbs - peppermint, anise, camomile, or, as do the Swedish women, use pine needles or birch leaves. Put the herbs in a pot of water and bring to a rolling boil. Remove the pot from the burner to a convenient location. Wait several minutes to allow the temperature of the steam to reach a comfortable level. Place your head over the pot, high enough over the water so that your skin will feel comfortably warm, not hot. Cover your head with a big bath towel, and steam your face for about 3 to 5 minutes. Turn your face so that every part of it, as well as your neck will receive the benefit of this aromatic facial bath.

The herbal steam of distilled water combined with the oils of the herbs, will cleanse your face thoroughly, open pores, loosen old stale makeup, blackheads, dirt, and make your complexion soft and beautifully clean.

Following the facial sauna, rinse your face with cool water for approximately one minute. Pat dry gently with a soft cloth.

Dry Brush Massage

For centuries, Scandinavian countries have used saunas and steambaths for their revitalizing effects. Saunas are still found in the typical Swedish home today and are used often by most Swedes. Following the traditional Sauna, Swedes are in the habit of vigorously rubbing their bodies dry with a towel, and then following with a soft brush massage. This is a very beneficial practice since it stimulates the skin to increase cell regeneration.

The skin is as important as the kidneys in

cleansing and detoxifying the body. When the skin becomes clogged and inactive, its pores remain choked with dead cells, uric acid, and other impurities.

The dry brush massage is very simple to do and takes only 10 minutes. Use either a soft natural fiber brush, a loofa, or a rough towel and beginning with the feet, brush vigorously using circular motions and continue up the legs brushing the entire body in the same manner. This action releases the impurities in your skin, opens clogged pores, and stimulates cell growth, thereby increasing the skin's vitality and giving skin a beautiful healthy glow. Follow with a warm and cold shower to rinse off the dead skin particles.

Benefits of Dry Brush Massage

- It will stimulate and increase blood circulation in all underlying organs and tissues, and especially in the small blood capillaries of your skin.
- It will revitalize and increase the eliminative capacity of your skin and help to throw toxins out of the system.
- It will stimulate the hormone and oil producing glands.
- It will have a powerful rejuvenating influence on the nervous system by stimulating nerve endings in the skin.

- It will contribute to a healthier muscle tone and better distribution of fat deposits.
- It will make you feel better all over.
- It will improve your health generally, and help prevent premature aging.

Important Tips on the Dry Brush Massage

- Be sure to clean your brush following each use.
- Avoid brushing the parts of your skin that are irritated, infected, or damaged in any way.
- The facial skin is too sensitive for brushing, therefore it is better to use the Swedish facial sauna for the face.
- If your skin is dry and shows signs of premature aging, follow the massage with a body rub using the Formula F-Plus oil. If there are no signs of premature aging or skin disorders, a lighter, less theraputic oil may be preferred. In this case, almond oil can be used as a body rub. Almond oil is a finely grained, very light oil and absorbs quickly to soften the skin.

Chapter 4

Natural Internal Cosmetics

Here are a few ways you can improve your complexion and enhance your natural beauty internally - Swedish Style - in your own home.

Rose Hip Tea

1 T. dried rose hips or rose hip powder
1 cup water
honey to taste

Use one tablespoon of dried rose hips or rose hip powder for each cup of water. Steep in hot water for 5 minutes (for powder) or 15 minutes (for whole or halves). Strain, sweeten with honey, and enjoy a vitamin C-loaded, nutritious and beautifying pink-colored tea.

Swedish Beauty Secrets

Imported Scandinavian rose hips and rose hip powder may be bought in the health food stores or import shops.

Swedish Rose Hip Soup

2 T. rose hip powder
1 cup water
½ T. corn starch or potato flour

Use 2 tablespoons of rose hip powder to one cup of water for each serving. Boil in pan for 5 minutes. Sweeten with honey and thicken with a half tablespoon of corn starch or potato flour per serving. Also, soybean flour could be used to make the soup even more nutritious. After adding the thickening, boil again for 3 minutes. Serve warm or chilled. Can be served with sweet milk or cream, and sprinkled with wheat germ, crushed raw nuts, or sunflower seeds. An excellent, beautifying dessert!

Note: never use aluminum or copper utensils when cooking rose hips. Not only does copper and aluminum destroy vitamin C on contact, but the acids of rose hips can dissolve the aluminum and you will be eating toxic residues of it with your food. Always use glass, or stainless steel utensils in your food preparation.

Rose Hip Puree

1 lb. fresh rose hips
1 pint water
honey to taste

If you live in the northern parts of the country and can gather your own rose hips in the fall, here's how you can make rose hip puree from fresh rose hips.

Remove the stalks and the blossom ends of the berries. Wash quickly in cold water. Cut or break berries in half and remove the seeds and the "hair" from the shells with your fingers. Use one pound of rose hips for each pint of water. Bring to a boil and simmer for about 10 to 15 minutes. Then press through a sieve, or mix in a blender. Serve hot or cold. Sweeten with honey.

ROSE HIP TABLETS

You can buy rose hip tablets from the health food stores. Read the labels and note the vitamin C content of the tablets in milligrams. Take 500 milligrams a day with each meal, as a preventive dose. In conditions where the complexion needs improvement, doses of 1,500 to 3,000 milligrams daily should be used. Remember, Dr. Linus Pauling advises 3,000 to 6,000 mg. a day for optimum health and protection against diseases. To assure healthy collagen, the most important factor in the health of your skin and complexion, a minimum of 500 mg. a day should be taken. Even in these large doses, vitamin C is completely harmless and non-toxic.

WHEY

Unfortunately, it is difficult to obtain whey cheese and whey butter in the United States, as they are not produced here. However, I have succeeded in finding them occasionally in some better delicatessen shops, which specialize in European imports. Special cheese shops often sell Norwegian whey cheese made from goat milk, called *Jetmessöst*. If you can find whey cheese, buy it, for your health and beauty's sake, and eat it sliced as a regular cheese on your whole-grain sandwich. It is not only extremely beneficial, but delicious.

If you cannot get whey cheese, you can buy whey powder or whey tablets in most health food stores. They are just as beneficial.

Take 2 tablespoons of whey in a glass of fruit juice or skim milk each morning and again before retiring. Whey powder could be also used in baking, cooking, added to soups or cereals, etc. I add whey powder to my yogurt or acidophilus milk.

Chapter 5

Natural External Cosmetics

The cosmetics described here are easy to make in your own kitchen from natural ingredients which you can buy in your grocery store, drugstore, or health food store. They are completely non-allergenic and would not harm the most delicate skins. They are simple and inexpensive. But don't be deceived by their simplicity. They are biologically more effective than most commercial cosmetics, regardless of price. They will improve your complexion and make your skin look younger, smoother and lovelier.

Since all ingredients in the following recipes are 100% natural and no preservatives are used, they will easily lose their freshness. Therefore you should prepare the amount which will best suit your needs. Feel free to reduce the recipes if needed. Remember to store the cosmetics in the refrigerator.

All of the oils mentioned may be obtained from health food stores. However, in order for these oils to have the maximum beneficial effect on your skin, they should be natural, unprocessed, cold-pressed and fresh. It may be difficult to find such oils, so read the labels carefully. Some oils, even in the natural food stores, are labeled "cold-processed", which means that a chemical extraction method has been used. Please use only those oils labeled "cold-pressed" and make certain they are free from preservatives. It is best to purchase only the amount of oil that you will use within a month or two because, like all fresh foods, oils will become rancid very quickly. Please store all oils in the refrigerator to inhibit rancidity.

Formula F

5 T. sesame oil
4 T. avocado oil
3 T. olive oil
2 T. almond oil

Mix oils together and shake well. Apply a few drops to your face, neck, hands and arms and massage it gently into your skin. Then dry off the excess with a soft cotton ball. This will remove all the impurities, dead skin cells and the stale residues of old cosmetics.

This natural cosmetic, mixed from the most beautifying oils known to man, will do wonders for your skin. It will make your skin moist and soft, young and beautiful.

Formula F Plus

2 T. sesame oil
2 T. avocado oil
1 T. olive oil
1 T. almond oil
10,000 I.U. vitamin E
200,000 USP units vitamin A

Pour the oils into an empty bottle or small jar. Use 10 gelatine capsules of vitamin E (1,000 I.U. each) and 8 capsules of vitamin A (25,000 units each). Puncture the capsules with a needle, or cut the ends off with scissors, and squeeze the contents into the bottle. Shake well. Apply gently to the skin where needed and massage with fingertips. Remove excess with a soft cotton ball. Keep refrigerated.

I composed this Formula specifically for those who have badly deteriorated complexions and a prematurely aged skin, covered with wrinkles and blemishes. The healing and beautifying oils of Formula F Plus, fortified with vitamins A and E, will feed your skin with the nutrients it needs and help to revitalize and restore its normal activity. Use this Formula intermittently with the regular Formula F; one month of regular Formula F, the next month Formula F Plus, and so on.

You will be amazed at the rejuvenative effect Formula F Plus will have on your complexion, if used regularly.

Formula F Cream

$1/4$ cup sesame oil
$1/8$ cup avocado oil
$1/8$ cup almond oil
1 fresh egg yolk
$1/2$ tsp. apple cider vinegar

Place the eggs in a bowl and beat with a rotary beater until thick. Mix the oils in a cup and add slowly to the eggs and continue beating. When smooth, add the vinegar and beat a little more. Keep in a jar tightly covered, in the refrigerator. This cream is excellent for dry, rough skin. It is rich in lecithin, vitamin A and poly-unsaturated oils. It will make your skin soft and moist.

Cucumber Astringent

1 cup fresh cucumber juice
$1/4$ tsp. honey

Using a blender or food processor, pulverize the cucumber. The cucumber may also be grated if no blender or food processor is available. Place the pulverized cucumber in a square of cheese cloth and press through to make the juice. Pour the juice and honey into an empty bottle and shake well. Apply with a cotton pad on your face and neck and let it dry.

Leave it on over night, if desired, or use as a base under makeup. Store in refrigerator. After a few days make a fresh batch.

Cucumbers contain natural vegetable hormones which are very benefical for your skin. Cucumber is also a natural, harmless skin tightener, or astringent. It will do wonders to your wrinkles and lines. Cucumber has been used extensively in Sweden and Germany as an active ingredient in commercially manufactured cosmetics. In more recent years manufacturers in the U.S. have also been using cucumber as an ingredient in cosmetics. Honey is known for its skin softening properties and helps to retain moisture.

Cucumber Beauty Mask

1 small cucumber
1/4 cup skim milk
1/2 tsp. honey
1 tsp. crushed ice

Cut the cucumber into 1 inch pieces and mix in an electric mixer with the skim milk, honey, and the ice to a consistency of porridge. Don't let the blender run too long so that the formula becomes too liquid.

Apply generously all over the face, neck and hands. Lie down for ten or fifteen minutes, then wash off with cold water. This is a good moisturizer for oily skin.

Honey Moisturizer

1 T. honey
1 cup cold water
1/2 tsp. lemon juice or apple cider

Dissolve the honey in the cold water. Add lemon juice or apple cider vinegar.

Apply with a cotton pad freely to your face, neck and arms, especially after a bath. Leave it on and let it dry. It will moisturize and soften your skin and help to restore the natural acid mantel to the skin, disturbed by the bath. Honey is a natural *humectant*, or skin softener. Beauty-conscious Swedish women have used honey as a cosmetic for centuries.

Honey-Egg Mask

1 egg white
1/2 tsp. honey

Beat the egg white with honey and apply to your face and neck liberally. Leave it on for about 10 to 15 minutes, then wash off with cold water without soap. This simple beauty mask will startle you with the most amazing results. Albumin of egg white is a natural astringent. It will draw your skin together and tighten it. Honey is a wonderful moisturizer and a softener. Together they work miracles on your skin.

Oatmeal Mask

1/4 cup rolled oats
1/2 cup buttermilk

Finely grind rolled oats using a blender or food processor and then combine with buttermilk. Let set in the refrigerator for 1 hour. Massage the mask liberally onto your face and leave on for 25 minutes. Rinse with cool water and notice the amazing results. This mask helps to reduce enlarged pores and deep-cleans the complexion.

Wheat Germ Mask

1 T. yogurt
1 T. raw wheat germ

Mix well and apply to a clean face. Gently massage this formula into your skin for 5 minutes and rinse off with cool water. This formula will revitalize your skin and moisturize oily skin, giving it a healthy glow.

Egg Mask

1 egg white

Beat 1 egg white with a mixer until very foamy, but not stiff. Brush on with a shaving brush all over the face and neck. Leave on for 20 minutes. Remove with cool water.

This is a very simple but very beneficial mask, used to close large pores and tighten skin.

Milk and Honey Cleansing Mask

1 egg white
1 tsp. fat free dry milk
$1/2$ tsp. honey

Mix all ingredients well and apply in a thick layer to the face. Relax for 20 minutes. Remove with warm water, followed with a cool rinse. This is a highly astringent cleanser that diminishes large pores and is wonderful for oily skin.

Apple Cider Skin Freshener

8 T. water
1 T. apple cider vinegar

Combine the ingredients and you now have a simple skin freshener that will restore the ph-balance of your skin and make your skin feel soft and lovely. Use this freshener as a final rinse following cleansing and to remove final traces of masks. Store this freshener in the refrigerator.

Oily Skin Astringent

*1 oz. peppermint
(dried and crushed)
1 oz. camomile (dried and crushed)
1 T. cider vinegar
3 T. water*

Boil water and remove from heat. Add the herbs and let steep 10 minutes and then strain. Let the teas cool and then add the cider vinegar. Apply with a cotton ball to oily areas.

Almond Skin Cleanser for Oily Skin

*1 cup almonds
2 T. plain yogurt
1 tsp. lemon juice*

Grind the almonds in the blender or food processor until finely ground. Mix with yogurt and lemon juice into a paste. Use this mixture to cleanse the face. Be sure to rub lightly over oily part of the skin and follow with a warm rinse, then finish by using a cool rinse.

Swedish Beauty Secrets

These skin care methods are all very beneficial for the skin, but remember, all the skin care products combined, cannot hide the effects of poorly nourished skin. Your skin needs good circulation, good nerve function, and a ready supply of nutrients, to aid its rapid growth so your skin can look healthier, more beautiful, and stay younger longer.

Chapter 6

Beauty From Within

Because beauty comes from within, you must realize the importance of feeding not only your skin, internally and externally, but also feeding your whole body so that you can enjoy optimum health. Glowing good looks is, more than anything else, a reflection of inner vitality, vibrant health and unclouded happiness. The royal road to health and beauty is optimum nutrition.

Therefore, it will be most appropriate to end this book with my favorite dish, *Fruit Salad a la Airola*. This is not only a most delicious dish, but it is the most nutritious and perfectly balanced meal I know. It is a storehouse of high-grade proteins and all the essential vitamins, minerals, essential fatty acids and enzymes you need for optimum health. This salad should be a daily must for the beauty-conscious and health conscious alike.

Fruit Salad a la Airola

1 bowl fresh fruits, organically grown if possible
1 handful raw nuts, and or sunflower seeds
3-4 soaked prunes or a handful of raisins, unsulphured
3 T. cottage cheese, preferably homemade, unsalted
1 T. raw wheat germ
3 T. yogurt
1 T. wheat germ oil
2 tsp. natural raw honey
1 tsp. fresh lemon juice

Wash and dry all fruits carefully. Use any available fruits and berries, but try to get at least three or four different kinds. Peaches, grapes, pears, papaya, bananas, and fresh pineapple are particularly good for producing a delightful bouquet of rich, penetrating flavors. A variety of colors will make the salad festive and attractive.

Chop or slice the bigger fruits, but leave grapes and berries whole. Place them in a large bowl and add prunes and nuts (nuts and sunflower seeds could be crushed or ground). Make a dressing with one teaspoon honey (or more if most of the fruits used are sour), one teaspoon of lemon juice, and two tablespoons of water. Pour over the fruit, add wheat germ, and toss well. Mix cottage cheese, yogurt, wheat germ oil, and one teaspoon of honey in a separate cup until it is fairly smooth in texture and pour it on top of the salad. Sprinkle with nuts and sunflower seeds, serve at once.

This salad is not only the most nutritious dish in the world, but it is indeed, a most beneficial internal cosmetic.

You have now learned how to look and feel healthier, younger and more beautiful - the Swedish way - with internal and external natural cosmetics which you can make in your own kitchen. You can use the recommended recipes and formulas with confidence. They have all been time-tested through actual use in Sweden and other parts of the world. They have also been proven to be extremely beneficial and effective by many beauty consultants. All suggested ingredients - sesame oil, avocado oil, almond oil, olive oil, honey, cucumber, eggs, apple cider vinegar, milk, oatmeal, brewers yeast, almonds, lemon juice, and wheat germ - are all used as active ingredients in many cosmetic formulas by known cosmetic manufacturers throughout the world. Natural and botanical cosmetics have been researched extensively and are gaining increased popularity as more and more women discover their beauty-enhancing qualities.

Natural cosmetics are wonderful beauty aids and cost very little. They will do wonders for your complexion and will enhance your natural beauty. Do not forget, however, that in the final analysis, beauty comes from within. If you fail to feed your skin from within and keep your collagen healthy and your eliminative tract clean and the assimilation of nutrients effective, then even the most wonderful natural cosmetic, applied externally, would be of little benefit. This is why Swedish beauty secrets - rose hips and whey - are so important. This is also why it is necessary to follow an optimum diet of health building foods. All of these things will be miraculous improvers of your general health. Better health will reflect itself in the way you look.

By participating in the total program of Swedish beauty care as outlined in this book you can expect the most remarkable results. You will indeed feel and look <u>healthier</u>, <u>younger</u>, and more <u>beautiful</u>.

ABOUT THE AUTHOR

Paavo Airola, Ph.D., N.D., is an internationally-recognized nutritionist, naturopathic physician, educator, and award-winning author. Raised and educated in Europe, he studied biochemistry, nutrition, and natural healing in biological medical centers of Sweden, Germany, and Switzerland. He lectures extensively world-wide, both to professionals and laymen, holding yearly educational seminars for physicians. He has been a visiting lecturer at many universities and medical schools, including the Stanford University Medical School.

Dr. Paavo Airola is the author of fourteen widely-read books, notably his two international best-sellers, **How to Get Well**, and **Are You Confused? How to Get Well** is the most authoritative and practical manual on natural healing in print. It is used as a textbook in several universities and medical schools, and regarded as a reliable reference manual, the "Bible of Natural Healing," by doctors, researchers, nutritionists, and students of health and holistic healing. Dr. Airola's book, **Hypoglycemia: A Better Approach**, has revolutionized the therapeutic concept of this insidious, complex, and devastating affliction. The American Academy of Public Affairs issued Dr. Airola the Award of Merit for his book on arthritis.

Dr. Airola's monumental work, **Everywoman's Book**, is a great new contribution in the field of holistic medicine. It not only confirms Dr. Airola's unchallenged leadership in the field of nutrition and holistic healing, but demonstrates his genius as an original thinker, philosopher, and profound humanitarian.

The Airola Diet & Cookbook is Dr. Airola's newest book. It contains not only 300 delicious and nutritious recipes and Dr. Airola's Weight Loss Program, but also the most thorough presentation to date of the scientific basis for the Airola Optimum Diet — the world-famous diet of supernutrition for superhealth.

Dr. Airola is President of the International Academy of Biological Medicine; a member of the International Naturopathic Association; and a member of the International Society for Research on Civilization Diseases and Environment, the prestigious Forum for world-wide research founded by Dr. Albert Schweitzer. Dr. Airola is listed in the **Directory of International Biography, The Blue Book, The Men of Achievement, Who's Who in American Art, Who's Who in the West,** and **Canadian Who's Who.**

LET THESE TIMELY, INFORMATIVE, AND AUTHORITATIVE BOOKS BY

Dr. Paavo Airola

AMERICA'S #1 BESTSELLING HEALTH AUTHOR

GUIDE YOU TO VIBRANT HEALTH, YOUTHFUL VITALITY, AND LONG LIFE.

1. **HOW TO GET WELL. Foreword by H. Rudolph Alsleben, M.D.** $14.95
   The most treasured manual on natural healing in print. Proven and effective treatments for our most common ailments, with special diets, vitamins, herbs, etc. A *must* for doctors, researchers, and health students. Used as a textbook in many universities. #1 international health bestseller. Over 700,000 hardcover copies sold! Clothbound. 300 pages. Indexed.

2. **ARE YOU CONFUSED? Foreword by Leslie H. Salov, M.D.** $7.95
   The more you read about health and nutrition — the more confused you are? Read this revolutionary and pioneering eye-opener. It will de-confuse your mind on diets, proteins, supplements, fasting, milk, distilled water, etc. Considered by doctors and critics to be "The most important health book ever published." 224 pages.

3. **EVERYWOMAN'S BOOK. Foreword by Mary Ann Kibler, M.D.**
   A monumental and comprehensive guide on every aspect of women's health from preconception to maturity. Natural childbirth, infant and child feeding, childhood diseases, female health problems, sexual disorders, beauty and longevity secrets. 640 pages of priceless information compiled by the world-famous health authority in collaboration with a board of leading medical experts. A *must* for every woman concerned with her and her family's health. Illustrated, indexed, referenced.

   Clothbound edition $17.95
   Quality softback edition $12.95

4. **THE AIROLA DIET AND COOKBOOK. Co-author: Anni M. Lines, R.D.** $12.95
   Dr. Airola's masterpiece with over 300 nutritious and delicious recipes. The scientific basis of the Airola Diet — the world-famous diet of supernutrition for superhealth — is presented in more detail than in any other of his books. Includes Dr. Airola's Weight Loss Program — the only reducing diet that takes pounds off while improving your health. Illustrated, indexed, hardcover, luxury edition. 288 pages.

5. **HYPOGLYCEMIA: A BETTER APPROACH** $7.95
   A revolutionary diet and common-sense approach that successfully eliminates the syndrome of low blood sugar while improving the general health.

6. **HOW TO KEEP SLIM, HEALTHY, AND YOUNG WITH JUICE FASTING** .. $5.95
   The most complete, authoritative, and up-to-date fasting book available. Used as guide in fasting clinics around the world. Detailed hour-by-hour instructions.

7. **WORLDWIDE SECRETS OF STAYING YOUNG** $6.95
   Proven ways to reverse the aging processes and stay younger longer. Based on Dr. Airola's world-wide travels and research.

8. **CANCER: CAUSES, PREVENTION, AND TREATMENT —
   THE TOTAL APPROACH** $3.95
   Nutritional and other alternative therapies. Fully documented.

9. **STOP HAIR LOSS** $2.95
   Nutritional and other means to stimulate hair growth.

10. **SWEDISH BEAUTY SECRETS** $3.95
    Feel and look healthier, younger, and more beautiful — at any age. Recipes and Formulas.

11. **THE MIRACLE OF GARLIC** $3.95
    World-wide scientific studies reveal the amazing nutritional and medicinal properties of garlic.

(Prices subject to change without notice)

AVAILABLE AT ALL LEADING HEALTH FOOD STORES AND BOOK STORES
or directly from:

HEALTH PLUS, Publisher,   P.O. Box 1027   Sherwood, Oregon 97140